Miracle Hour

A method of prayer that will change your life

by
Linda Schubert

Foreword by Rev. Robert DeGrandis, S.S.J.

Nihil obstat: Kevin P. Joyce, Ph.D., *Censor deputatus*

Imprimatur: +Pierre DuMaine, Bishop of San Jose, CA
January 24, 1992

48th Printing — January 2015

Cover photograph by Michael Powers
Half Moon Bay, CA

All Scripture quotations are taken from
the New International Version

ISBN 0-9632643-0-3

Linda Schubert
Miracles of the Heart Ministries
P.O. Box 4034
Santa Clara, CA 95056
Telephone (408) 734-8663
Fax (408) 734-8661
Web site: www.linda-schubert.com
E-mail linda@linda-schubert.com

Foreword

In my travels around the world ministering to priests, religious and laity, I am always challenging people to pray. I have heard countless stories of miraculous turnarounds of desperate circumstances when Christians begin to seriously pray. During my "Healing Power of Holy Orders" priest retreats I encourage the priests to be faithful to a daily holy hour. I am called to spend a minimum of two hours a day in prayer. I could not do the work to which the Lord has called me without this time with Him. Bishop Fulton Sheen, probably the most influential American Catholic priest in history, made a vow at ordination to spend an hour a day before the Blessed Sacrament. He was faithful to that commitment until the day he died. Sister Briege McKenna, O.S.C., who spends three hours a day in prayer, has one of the most powerful healing ministries in the world. You will find that those who are truly doing the Lord's work are committed to daily prayer. They know how powerless they are without God's grace. When we die and face our Lord I am convinced that we will never be sorry for the time spent in prayer. Most often, people on their deathbeds regret the lack of time spent in prayer.

I believe this booklet, *Miracle Hour*, will be of great help not only to beginners but also to those in a mature walk with the Lord who struggle with their prayer time.

It's a very balanced and effective approach to prayer that I highly recommend. Some of the prayers are condensed from books I have written, and are used with permission.

May our Lord Jesus Christ bless you now, with a new gift of prayer.

Rev. Robert DeGrandis, S.S.J.
New Orleans, LA

Acknowledgment

Many people helped me, directly and indirectly, as this booklet began to take shape. Many years ago I attended a seminar with Dick Eastman, the author of *The Hour That Changes the World*. That book was a significant inspiration in the development of *Miracle Hour*. I also want to acknowledge the work of Father Robert DeGrandis, S.S.J. The format of the prayer on forgiveness in *Miracle Hour* is an adaptation of his prayer. The Ephesians 1:4 Prayer Community in Dublin, California, gave me permission to incorporate the Litany of Praise, which is a favorite of many. Everything I write is passed around to many readers in the formative stages, with each adding suggestions and insight. The work is enriched by all of their contributions. May the Lord bless each contributor in a very special way, and return to them a hundredfold for their generosity.

Miracle Hour

" ...Could you not keep watch for one hour?"
(Mark 14:37).

Do you have trouble with commitment to prayer? Sometimes I go for long periods of time with a rich, full prayer life, then it slips away and for months I struggle to regain that intimacy and depth with the Lord. This booklet emerged at the end of a long dry time, when I was so ashamed of my prayerlessness that I cried out to the Lord for help. I woke up one morning and yelled at the Lord, "I HAVE TO have a quality hour with You! I can only do it with Your grace. Please, *please* help me!"

He not only gave me a rich, grace-filled hour, but also showed me a simple format for a daily hour that would draw me into deeper intimacy with Him and empower me in my Christian walk. Remember the old saying, "Inch by inch it's a cinch"? How about five minutes by five minutes it's a cinch? I have divided the hour into 12 five-minute segments, as shown in the "clock" on the next page.

"Morning by morning, O Lord, you hear my voice; morning by morning I lay my requests before you and wait in expectation" (Psalm 5:3).

Between the five-minute segments you might want to pray the "Our Father," or another brief prayer of your choice. For Catholics or others with a relationship with

1

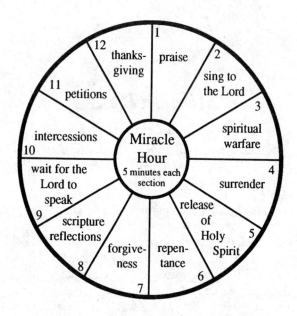

Miracle Hour
5 minutes each section

1 praise
2 sing to the Lord
3 spiritual warfare
4 surrender
5 release of Holy Spirit
6 repentance
7 forgiveness
8 scripture reflections
9 wait for the Lord to speak
10 intercessions
11 petitions
12 thanksgiving

the mother of Jesus, I would invite the inclusion of a "Hail Mary" as a transition between the sections. For those who pray in the charismatic gift of tongues, I would encourage that form of prayer at various times throughout the hour.

It's wonderful to start the day with the Lord, praying in the early hours before work begins. Having a set time and place for prayer has positive benefits, whether it is morning, noon or night. Ideally, prayer should overflow from that formal time into spontaneous encounters with God all day long. It is marvelous when we can come into a freedom where the Lord is so real that we have "prayer conversations" with Him in the context of all our activities.

The prayers and reflections in this booklet are offered as suggestions to help you get started. The more you can personalize them, and allow the Holy Spirit to lead you spontaneously in your own words, the more meaningful it will be. You can expect a tremendous awakening and continual deepening of your spiritual life through this daily "Miracle Hour." A friend, Ginny, who reviewed an early draft of this booklet, commented: "This is going to take people through a process of breaking down barriers and loosening things up in many areas of their lives." When I showed it to another friend, Nancy, she said, "We've been praying for someone to do this!" The scriptures for additional study at the end of each section were her idea.

I encourage you to come to prayer with an attitude of openness and expectancy. Come remembering all the ways God has helped you in the past, and come expecting Him to help you even more in the future. Consider the "Miracle Hour" as an intensely loving "power encounter" with your heavenly Father. It's a time of cleansing, deeper consecration and growth in understanding of the ways of God. Come accepting and expecting His love. Come prepared to experience His goodness and mercy. Come with a yielded heart that says simply, "Lord, change me." Come to be transformed, loosened up, healed and empowered.

There is such a desperate need for people of prayer in this world of atheism and anti-Christian practices. I believe God is calling His people to prayer more intensely than ever before. If we could only comprehend the immensity of God's plan for our lives, and the importance of our prayers, we would stop in our tracks and reevaluate our priorities immediately. Life is just too short and too precious to waste on empty things. As I write this I am thinking of my beloved brother-in-law, Harvell Smith (to whom I dedicate this booklet), who was killed in an airplane crash in the Caribbean. He had perhaps a minute or two to get his life right with God. None of us know how many days, weeks or months we have left in this precious life. In 1984 I had a mastectomy for breast cancer, and had to face the possibility of death. It turned my life around and I made a decision not to waste another moment on empty things. Will you join me today, and make a new commitment to be a person of prayer? God will bless you for it. Get a Bible, a note pad and a pen, and find a quiet place. Join me now, in an "hour of power" that will change your life.

"Loving heavenly Father we ask for a spirit of prayer to come upon us now. Increase our longing for You, and our longing for the salvation of people around the world. I pray with the psalmist, *'As the deer pants for streams of water, so my soul pants for You, O God. My soul thirsts for God, for the living God. When can I go and meet with God?'* (Psalm 42:1-2) Come Holy Spirit, I want to meet with God. Please teach me how to pray. In Jesus' name. Amen."

(Mk 1:35, 1 Ti 6:19, Ps 119:147, Lk 2:37, Ps 55:17, Eph 3:14-21, Eph 1:15-23, Ps 57:8, Jos 5:14-15, Ps 95:6, Ps 96:9, Jn 4:14, Is 2:3, Ps 27:4, Ps 122:1, Ps 123:1, 1 Ti 2:8, Lk 11:1, Ps 34:15, Is 65:24, Ps 94:9, Ja 5:4, 1 Pe 3:12)

LET US PRAY!

(Five minutes per section)

1. **PRAISE**: *"Praise the Lord, O my soul; all my inmost being, praise His holy name"* (Psalm 103:1). Throughout scripture, God is very insistent about praise. I suspect we have much to learn about the amazing, mysterious power of this humble activity. When we praise we seem to be acknowledging His supremacy and authority

in our lives. Through praise we are stating that we are weak and He is strong. Praise makes room in our hearts for God's will to be done, and recognizes the absurdity of any attempt to manipulate God in prayer. He is sovereign. This awesome Creator, who loves us so much that He sent Jesus to die for us that we might have a place in His family, deserves our adoration and praise. His love for us is outrageous, beyond comprehension.

There is something special about people who praise. They have a bright light in their eyes that reflects something beyond themselves. People of praise are people of faith. Their very lives state to the world that they trust their loving heavenly Father, know He intends goodness for His children, and expect extravagant answers to prayer.

The very "sacrifice" of praise – working at it when we don't feel like it – draws us into the presence of the Lord. People of praise discover that this action of the heart, the mind (and sometimes just the will) is very healthy for body, mind and spirit. Praise draws us into a healthy mental attitude. Praise increases our capacity to live and grow in love and holiness. Praise draws us into the abundant life in which God created us to live. Let us praise God in all things!

Read *aloud* the following litany of praise and allow it to open your spirit and draw you into the realm of the miraculous. For the next five minutes just forget about yourself and concentrate on God. He is awesome! (5 minutes)

LITANY OF PRAISE

Praise You, Jesus, You are my Life, my Love.
Praise You, Jesus, You are the Name above all names.
Praise You, Jesus, You are Emmanuel, God with us.
Praise You, Jesus, You are the King of kings.
Praise You, Jesus, You are the King of creation.
Praise You, Jesus, You are King of the universe.
Praise You, Jesus, You are the Lord of lords.
Praise You, Jesus, You are the Almighty.
Praise You, Jesus, You are the Christ.
Praise You, Jesus, You are Christ, the King.
Praise You, Jesus, You are the Lamb of God.
Praise You, Jesus, You are the Lion of Judah.
Praise You, Jesus, You are the Bright Morning Star.
Praise You, Jesus, You are our Champion and Shield.
Praise You, Jesus, You are our Strength and our Song.
Praise You, Jesus, You are the Way for our life.
Praise You, Jesus, You are the only Truth.
Praise You, Jesus, You are the Real Life.
Praise You, Jesus, You are the Wonderful Counselor.
Praise You, Jesus, You are the Prince of Peace.
Praise You, Jesus, You are the Light of the World.
Praise You, Jesus, You are the Living Word.
Praise You, Jesus, You are our Redeemer.
Praise You, Jesus, You are the Messiah.
Praise You, Jesus, You are the Anointed One.
Praise You, Jesus, You are the Holy One of Israel.
Praise You, Jesus, You are the Good Shepherd.
Praise You, Jesus, You are the Sheepgate.
Praise You, Jesus, You are the Lord of hosts.
Praise You, Jesus, You are the Rock of all ages.
Praise You, Jesus, You are my Hiding Place.
Praise You, Jesus, You are the Savior of the World.

Praise You, Jesus, You are the Strong Tower.
Praise You, Jesus, You are the Mountain Refuge.
Praise You, Jesus, You are the Bread of Life.
Praise You, Jesus, You are the Font of all holiness.
Praise You, Jesus, You are the Living Water.
Praise You, Jesus, You are the True Vine.
Praise You, Jesus, You are my Spouse, my Maker.
Praise You, Jesus, You are our Fortress.
Praise You, Jesus, You are the Deliverer.
Praise You, Jesus, You are our Victory.
Praise You, Jesus, You are our Salvation.
Praise You, Jesus, You are our Righteousness.
Praise You, Jesus, You are our Wisdom.
Praise You, Jesus, You are our Sanctification.
Praise You, Jesus, You are our Justification.
Praise You, Jesus, You are the Door.
Praise You, Jesus, You are the great I AM.
Praise You, Jesus, You are the great High Priest.
Praise You, Jesus, You are the Cornerstone.
Praise You, Jesus, You are the Sure Foundation.
Praise You, Jesus, You are our Joy.
Praise You, Jesus, You are our Portion and Cup.
Praise You, Jesus, You are my Healing and Wholeness.
Praise You, Jesus, You are our Covenant.
Praise You, Jesus, You are the Promise of the Father.
Praise You, Jesus, You are the Everlasting One.
Praise You, Jesus, You are the Most High God.
Praise You, Jesus, You are the Lamb that was slain.
Praise You, Jesus, You are the Just Judge.
Praise You, Jesus, You are the Balm of Gilead.
Praise You, Jesus, You are the Mighty Warrior.
Praise You, Jesus, You are my Defense.
Praise You, Jesus, You are the Bridegroom.
Praise You, Jesus, You are my Patience.

Praise You, Jesus, You are the Solid Reality.
Praise You, Jesus, You are my Provider.
Praise You, Jesus, You are the Resurrection and the Life.
Praise You, Jesus, You are the Alpha and the Omega.
Praise You, Jesus, You are the Beginning and the End.
Praise You, Jesus, You are all that I need.
Praise You, Jesus, You are all that I want.
Praise You, Jesus, You are worthy of all Praise!

(Ps 34:1, Mt 21:16, Jas 5:13, Ps 150:2, Ps 92:1-3, 2 Ch 20:22, Ps 35:28, Ps 51:15, 1 Pe 2:9, Mt 18:3, Ps 107:22, Heb 13:15, Ps 116:17, Rev 5:11-14, Rev 7:11-12, Rev 19:5)

(Our Father, etc.)

2. **SING TO THE LORD**: *"Come, let us sing for joy to the Lord; let us shout aloud to the Rock of our salvation. Let us come before Him with thanksgiving and extol Him with music and song"* (Psalm 95:102). It has been said that "He who sings, prays twice." Anointed music has a great power to open our spirits. Close your eyes, be still and allow music to rise up in your spirit. Hum, sing in tongues if you are released in that gift, or sing Christ-centered songs such as, "I Love You, Lord," "Turn Your Eyes Upon Jesus," the eightfold "Alleluia," etc., as the Holy Spirit leads you. (5 minutes)

(Ps 89:1, Ps 149:1, 1 Co 14:15, Eph 5:19, Col 3:16, Ps 63:5-7, Ps 90:14, Ps 40:3, 1 Ch 6:32, Ps 57:7, Ps 126:5, Is 12:6, Ps 100:2)

(Our Father, etc.)

3. **SPIRITUAL WARFARE:** *"Be strong in the Lord and in His mighty power. Put on the full armor of God so that you can take your stand against the devil's schemes..."* (Ephesians 6:12). The Bible reminds us that there are negative spiritual forces that can exert a controlling influence in our lives and diminish our capacity to be free, open and loving people. The Bible also reminds us that we have been given authority to come against the power of the enemy (Mark 16:17). Let's ask the Holy Spirit to make us wise and courageous in the use of that power.

At times in your life you may have inadvertently opened your spirit to some of those influences. It's time to close those doors. It is important when we pray to place ourselves specifically under the Lord's protection and take authority over any powers of evil. (This has already begun, because praise is one of the most powerful weapons against the enemy.) (5 minutes)

SPIRITUAL WARFARE PRAYER

Heavenly Father, I come before You in praise, worship and adoration. Thank You for sending Your Son Jesus to give me life, to give me forgiveness, to give me a place in Your family. Thank You for sending the Holy Spirit to guide me and empower me in my daily life. Heavenly Father, open my eyes that I may see Your greatness, Your majesty, Your victory on my behalf.

I place myself now under the cross of Jesus Christ and cover myself with the Precious Blood of Jesus. I surround myself with the light of Christ and say in the name of Jesus that nothing shall inter-

9

fere with the Lord's work being accomplished in my life.

I put on God's armor to resist the devil's tactics. I stand my ground with truth buckled around my waist and integrity for a breastplate. I carry the shield of faith to put out the burning arrows of the evil one. I accept salvation from God to be my helmet and receive the word of God from the Spirit to use as a sword (Ephesians 6:10,11,14,16,17).

Heavenly Father please show me any way that satan has a hold of my life. I let go of all those ways now. Any territory I have handed over to satan I now reclaim and place under the Lordship of Jesus Christ.

In the name of Jesus Christ I bind all spirits of the air, fire, water, ground, underground and nether world. I bind all forces of evil and claim the Blood of Jesus on the air, the atmosphere, the water, the ground and their fruits around us, the underground and the nether world. In the name of Jesus Christ I seal this room and all members of my family, relatives, associates and all sources of supply in the Blood of Jesus Christ. In the name of Jesus Christ I forbid every spirit from any source from harming me in any way.

In the name of Jesus Christ I reject the seductive lure of evil in all its forms and refuse to let sin have dominion over me. I reject satan and all his works and all his empty promises. Heavenly Father, I ask forgiveness for myself, my friends, relatives and ancestors for calling upon powers that set themselves up in opposition to Jesus Christ. I renounce

all openness to the occult, all false worship and all benefits from magical arts. I renounce every power apart from God and every form of worship that does not offer true honor to Jesus Christ. I specifically renounce_____.
(For example, astrology, fortune telling, crystals, tarot cards, ouija boards or any occult games, etc.) In the name of Jesus, I break any curses that may be coming against me or my family, and stop the transmission of those curses through my ancestry.

In the name of Jesus Christ, I bind you spirit of_____. (Ask the Lord to reveal the name. If you aren't sure about the name, identify it by its negative fruit: anger, unforgiveness, fear, insecurity, illness, trauma, etc.) I bind you away from me now, in Jesus' name. Lord Jesus, fill me with Your love to replace the fear; fill me with strength to replace the weakness, etc. (After each command, ask the Lord to fill you with the "positive opposite" of the negativity you removed: fear/love, illness/health, weakness/strength, etc.)

Loving Father, let the cleansing, healing waters of my baptism flow back through the generations to purify my family line of contamination. Thank You, Lord, for setting me free. *"...in all these things we are more than conquerors through Him who loved us"* (Romans 8:37). Spend a few moments in praise.

(Ro 13:12, 2 Cor 6:7, 1 Th 5:8, 1 Jn 4:1-6, 1 Th 5:21, 2 Co 4:4, Eph 2:2, Ac 26:18, 2 Th 2:9, Lk 9:42, 1 Pe 5:8-9, Eph 4:27, Ps 44:5, Lk 10:19, Ro 8:37, I Jn 5:5)

(Our Father, etc.)

4. **SURRENDER:** *"...who is willing to conse-crate himself today to the Lord?"* (1 Chronicles 29:5). Our healing and empowerment begins when we surrender to Jesus. People generally find that He is the strongest in them when they surrender, and are in a position of weakness before Him. There is nothing more important in your spiritual life than to say "Yes" to Jesus with all your heart and soul, and then to allow the Holy Spirit to work out the meaning of that "Yes" in your life. You can be 100% sure of this: God loves you (1 John 4:16) and will always be with you; and all His purposes for your life are good. The more we open up, yield, and simply allow ourselves to be drawn deeply into the Lord's love, the more our lives will come into right order. Will you say "Yes" to Jesus? You may have said "Yes" many times in your life, and yet today He may be calling you to go much deeper.

Once, after I had prayed the following prayer many times, the Lord asked, "Do you *really* mean it, Linda?" Shaken, I responded, "Yes, Lord," and He took me even deeper. Pray it now, from your heart. Pray it in your words, spontaneously, not as a ritual, but with an opening of yourself to God. (5 minutes)

A PRAYER OF SURRENDER

"...may Your will be done" (Matthew 26:42).

Loving Father, I surrender to You today with all my heart and soul. Please come into my heart in a deeper way. I say "Yes," to You today. I open all the secret places of my heart to You and say, "Come on in." Jesus You are Lord of my whole life. I believe in You and receive You as my Lord and Savior. I hold nothing back. Holy Spirit, bring me to deeper conversion to the person of Jesus Christ. I surrender all to You: my health, my family, my resources, occupation, skills, relationships, time management, successes and failures. I release it, and let it go. I surrender my understanding of how things ought to be, my choices and my will. I surrender to You the promises I have kept and the promises I have failed to keep. I surrender my weaknesses and strengths to You. I surrender my emotions, my fears, my insecurities, my sexuality. I especially surrender_____,

_____, _____.

(Continue to surrender other areas as the Holy Spirit reveals them to you.) Lord, I surrender my entire life to You, the past, the present and the future. In sickness and in health, in life and in death, I belong to You.

(If you know a song of surrender, you might close your eyes and sing it now. You could even make up a song spontaneously and sing it to Him.)

"Take, Lord, and receive, all my liberty, my memory, my understanding, and my entire will, all that I have and possess. You have given all to me. To You, O Lord, I return it. All is Yours. Dispose of it wholly according to Your will. Give me Your love and Your grace, for this is sufficient for me." (Prayer of St. Ignatius)

(Php 3:8, Pr 23:26, Ro 12:1, Mt 16:24, Lk 14:33, Ps 143:10, Ps 40:8, Dt 6:5, Pr 3:5, Jer 29:13, Jn 3:16, 1 Pe 1:18-19, Tit 3:5, Ro 10:9,13, Ro 1:6, Ro 14:8, Ac 16:30, 1 Jn 5:1,5)

5. **RELEASE OF THE HOLY SPIRIT:**

At Pentecost (Acts 2) the disciples devoted themselves to constant prayer until the Holy Spirit came upon them with tongues of fire, filled their lives and gave them courage and power to witness to the world. Some people call this release, or "baptism in the Holy Spirit," the "kiss of the Spirit." Its primary purpose is to empower Christians to bring Jesus to the world. Its primary effect is a tangible experience of the love of Jesus. (The hug of heaven!) Let us continually, daily, thank Him for a deeper release of the Holy Spirit in our own lives. Empowered by the Spirit we can change the world. One campus minister said about his ministry after the release of the Spirit, "Now, what I do, works!" According to Acts 2, this is normal Christianity. As you pray the following prayer, change it in some way to make it your own. (5 minutes)

PRAYER FOR RELEASE OF THE HOLY SPIRIT

"...you will receive power when the Holy Spirit comes on you, and you will be my witnesses...to the ends of the earth" (Acts 1:8).

Come Holy Spirit, and baptize me with the fire of Your love. I have surrendered to the best of my ability, and now I want to be filled with Your Spirit. I need Your power in my life. Please come, and fill me now. Lord, I believe that when I surrendered to You as Lord, we became one. You are the vine and I am a branch of the vine. All that You are is within me. My life flows from You. I believe that as I yield and ask, You will release Your strength, wisdom, healing, etc. to meet the needs of the hour. I yield now to receive Your sanctification gifts of Isaiah 11:2: wisdom and understanding, counsel and might, knowledge and the fear of the Lord. I need these gifts in my life, to grow as a Christian. I yield and ask You to release Your manifestation gifts of service, as listed in 1 Corinthians 12: wisdom, knowledge, faith, healing, miracles, prophecy, discernment, tongues and interpretation of tongues. I need them to witness to a hurting world. Only in Your power, guided by Your Spirit, can my life be fruitful. Holy Spirit come. Holy Spirit come. I want it all, wrapped in the greatest gift of all: *love*. *"...the greatest of these is love"* (1 Corinthians 13:13). Melt me, mold me, fill me, use me. Give me opportunities to use Your gifts to reveal Your love and mercy. Stretch me, Lord. I will not limit Your gifts by my perceptions of what I can handle. Holy Spirit, expand my capacity. Work in me in a powerful way. I want every purpose God has for my life to be fulfilled, and I need You, mighty Spirit of God, to bring that purpose to fulfillment. Come Holy Spirit. Come.

As You flow through me to minister to others, I know that You are flowing within me to heal my life too. Thank You for flooding the deep places of my life with Your electric love. Thank You for washing and cleansing any wounds and scars from the past that still have the power to dominate my thoughts and suppress my physical and emotional freedom. Thank You for bringing light into the shadows and warmth to any cold, dark rooms in my soul. Compassionate Holy Spirit thank You for coming and drawing out the uncried tears, the unfinished grieving, the pain of loss, the traumas, the fear, the emotional hurts so painful that they were "buried alive." Spirit of Wisdom thank You for coming into the root cause of any chronic failures. Gentle Holy Spirit, thank You for walking through my early years and facing the past with me. Thank You for reminding me that the love of Jesus was always there, filling in the gap between the love I needed and the love I received. (Thank the Holy Spirit for scanning your life and bringing to mind any hurtful memories that need to be healed. When they surface, say simply, "Holy Spirit I surrender that event to You for healing. Thank You for bringing Your good out of the hurt (Romans 8:28). Praise You, Jesus.") Let this be an opportunity for a deeper release of the Holy Spirit as more of your emotional life becomes unbound.

Thank You, Holy Spirit, for Your presence with me, flowing freely in me and through me. Thank You for being my friend, my teacher, my comforter, my counselor, my intercessor, and the giver of extravagant gifts. Thank You especially for_____. (Continue thanking Him spontaneously.)

Close your eyes and sing, "Come, Holy Ghost," or "Spirit of the Living God," or another song that invites the Holy Spirit to come. Amen.

(Ro 5:5, Joel 2:28, Mt 3:11, Lk 11:13, Jn 14:26, Gal 4:6, I Cor 2:13, Jn 16:13, Ro 8:11, Zec 4:6, Ac 2:2, Ro 8:9, 1 Co 3:16, Is 55:1, Mt 25:35-36, Mt 10:8, I Pe 4:10)

6. **REPENTANCE:** The more you are open to the Holy Spirit, the more aware you will be of those areas in your life where Jesus is not yet fully revealed in you. With that awareness should come a deep knowledge of the Lord's unconditional love. If you start feeling like a failure, remember the power of God's forgiving love, as expressed on the cross at Calvary. Then praise Him! Someone commented once that when we have sinned we can simply "Run to God, yell 'guilty!' and get on with things." This is a good reminder that we don't have to stay stuck and paralyzed with guilt. The Lord wants us to celebrate our movement toward Him. Sin has a power to hold us down and block the flow of God's love. We hide when we feel guilty. Repentance has a power to lift us up again and release the flow of God's love. *"But if we walk in the light, as he is in the light, we have fellowship with one another, and the blood of Jesus, his Son, purifies us from all sin"* (1 John 1:7). For Catholics (and those from other sacramental churches) the sacrament of reconciliation is one of the greatest gifts they can give themselves when they are faced with sin and guilt, especially when it is deep and heartfelt, and not ritualistic or superficial. Many are healed, emotionally and even physically, through this powerful instrument of grace. So this is a brief period of self-examination, of asking the Lord to reveal areas of unconfessed sin and then making some positive choices. The Lord may be calling you to speak with a pastor or with a wise, trusted friend. He may call you to make amends to a person you have harmed. Be obedient to what the Holy Spirit tells you to do. He won't ask you to do anything without giving you the strength to succeed.

As you pray the following prayer I am not recommending that you delve into all your sins and failings, but let the Holy Spirit guide you. Don't get bogged down in the details of the prayer, but use it to stimulate an active conscience. (5 minutes)

PRAYER OF REPENTANCE

" ...return to me with all your heart..." (Joel 2: 12).

Loving Father, I am sorry for all the ways I have offended You, knowingly or unknowingly. I have sinned in thought, word and deed. I have sinned in what I have done, and in what I have failed to do. I come before You and ask for the grace of a deeply repentant heart. You know my innermost secrets. I open my heart to You today and ask You to show me the ways I have blocked the flow of Your love. Forgive me, Father, for all my sins, faults and failings. For all the times I have gone astray and not chosen life, I am deeply sorry. I repent of lack of faith, acting in fear instead of faith, unbelief in Your goodness, or lack of truly believing in Your love for me.

I ask forgiveness for sins against purity: lust, fornication, adultery, unclean books, movies and videos and sexual fantasies, especially_____. I turn away from all those activities and I turn to You. I deeply repent of having an abortion or encouraging someone to have an abortion. Forgive me, Lord.

I repent of any compulsive, addictive behavior: drinking, drugs, gambling, sex, food and all addictions, especially_____. Thank

18

You, Father, for setting me free. I repent of not taking care of my physical and emotional health: lack of balance in nutrition, rest and exercise; perhaps the unhealthy suppression of emotions. I make a commitment today to take care of myself.

I'm sorry for the times I have hurt other people. I repent of any stealing, lying, deceiving and defrauding. I regret any lack of affirming others, brushing people off, coldness, unloving and inconsiderate behavior. I'm sorry for gossiping, betrayal of confidences and all breaches of faith. I repent of any envy, hatred, resentment, unforgiveness, jealousy, criticizing or judging others, not receiving love in the way it is offered, and withholding expressions of love. I especially ask forgiveness for_____.

I bring before You now those areas that I am the most ashamed to bring to You; areas that I have hidden, such as certain personal habits, secret guilt, dark areas I have previously refused to bring to You. I bring You all areas about which I am the most ashamed, especially_____.
Lord, I will no longer hide them from You, or from myself. Today is my day of healing and liberation.

Loving Father, what else should I bring to You? (Be still and listen.) For these offenses I beg pardon today. I accept Your forgiveness and now share Your forgiveness with others. Thank You, Lord. Amen.

(Ps 51:10, Ac 3:19, Pr 28:13, 1 Jn 1:9, 2 Ch 7:14, Is 55:7, Ac 2:38, Ps 51:17, Joel 2:13, Eph 5:11, 2 Cor 7:10, Ps 103:3, Ac 13:38, Eph 1:7, Heb 9:14, Ro 12:2, Mic 7:18, Lam 3:22, Rev. 22:14, Is 43:25, Ro 8:1,34, 1 Co 14:25, 1 Pe 1:16, 1 Th 4:3, Heb 10:10, Eph 5:11)

(Our Father, etc.)

7. **FORGIVENESS:** *"And when you stand praying, if you hold anything against anyone, forgive him, so that your Father in heaven may forgive you your sins"* (Mark 11:25). When Jesus is at the center of our lives we can expect His reconciliation within ourselves, and with others. The Holy Spirit will not let us off the hook in our broken relationships, nor will He expect us to forgive in our own power. He will do it through us, as we let Him.

Make a decision to be reconciled with the people in your life. Resolve to set them free, and set yourself free. Life is too short and too precious to waste being trapped and bound in the chains of unforgiveness. Let it go, today. You won't be sorry. Forgiveness begins with a decision; the emotions will follow.

A prayer covering some basic areas of life is included to help bring to mind buried anger, bitterness and resentment that need to be released through forgiveness. (As you slowly and reflectively pray the following prayer, pause quietly in each category and allow the Holy Spirit to bring specific people or situations to mind.) (5 minutes)

FORGIVENESS PRAYER

"In Him we have redemption through His blood, the forgiveness of sins, in accordance with the riches of God's grace that He lavished on us with all wisdom and understanding" (Ephesians 1:7-8).

Loving Father, I choose to forgive everyone in my life, including myself, because You have forgiven me. Thank You, Lord, for this grace. I forgive myself for all my sins, faults and failings, especially_____. I forgive myself for not being perfect, I accept myself and make a decision to stop picking on myself and being my own worst enemy. I release the things held against myself, free myself from bondage and make peace with myself today, by the power of the Holy Spirit.

I forgive my MOTHER for any negativity and unlove she may have extended to me throughout my life, knowingly or unknowingly, especially_____. For any abuse of any sort I do forgive her today. For any way that she did not provide a deep, full, satisfying mother's blessing I do forgive her today. I release her from bondage and make peace with her today.

I forgive my FATHER for any negativity and unlove he may have extended to me throughout my life, knowingly or unknowingly, especially_____. For any and all abuses, unkind acts, hurts, and deprivations I do forgive him today. For any way that I did not receive a full, satisfying father's blessing I forgive him today. I release him from bondage and make peace with him today.

I forgive my SPOUSE for any negativity and unlove extended throughout our time together, especially_____. For all the wounds of our relationship I do forgive my spouse today. I release my spouse from bondage and make peace between us today.

I forgive my CHILDREN for any hurts, especially_____. I release them from bondage and make peace with them today. Bless them, Lord.

I forgive my SISTERS and BROTHERS for any negativity and unlove, especially_____.
I forgive my BLOOD RELATIVES for any abuses, especially_____. I forgive my ANCESTORS for any negative actions that affect my life today and make it harder for me today to live in the freedom of a child of God. I release them from bondage and make peace with them today, in Jesus' name.

I forgive my FRIENDS for any actions of negativity and unlove, especially_____.
For any time they abused our relationship or led me astray, I do forgive them. I release them from all bondage and make peace with them today, in the power of the Holy Spirit.

I forgive my EMPLOYERS of the present and the past for any negativity and unlove, especially_____. I release them from all bondage and pray a blessing on them today, in Jesus' name.

I forgive all SCHOOL TEACHERS for any negative, abusive actions, especially_____.
I forgive LAWYERS, DOCTORS, NURSES, and other professionals, especially_____.
I forgive CLERGY and all representatives of the church, especially_____. I release them all, in Jesus' name.

I forgive every member of SOCIETY who has hurt me in any way; those who have hurt me by criminal action or who have harmed my family. I forgive all in public life who have passed laws opposing Christian values. I forgive all the unfair, anonymous sources of pain and annoyance in my life.

Heavenly Father I now ask for the grace to forgive the ONE PERSON IN LIFE WHO HAS HURT ME THE MOST. The one who is the hardest to forgive, I now choose to forgive, though I may still feel angry and hurt. I also make peace with the one family member, the one friend and the one authority figure who has hurt me the most.

Lord, is there anyone else I need to forgive? (Be still and listen.) Thank You, loving Father, for setting me free.

I now pray a blessing on those who have hurt me. Lord, do something special for each of them today. Thank You, Lord. I praise You. Amen.

(Lk 17:4, Eph 4:31-32, Col 3:13, Mt 6:14, Mt 5:44, Lk 6:35, Gal 5:14, I Th 3:12, I Pe 4:8, I Jn 4:12, Mt 26:28, 2 Ti 2:24, Tit 3:2, Jas 3:17, I Pe 1:22)

(Our Father, etc.)

8. **SCRIPTURE REFLECTIONS:** As I was browsing through scripture one morning the words, "Today I am freeing you from the chains on your wrists," leaped off the page from Jeremiah 40:4. I knew instantly that the Lord was saying He was releasing me to complete a difficult writing project about which I had been earnestly praying. I obviously took the phrase totally out of the original Biblical context, yet it was also obvious that the Lord

was using that verse to speak to me. As the days passed I began to experience a new freedom in writing.

Scripture is one of our most important avenues of interaction with the Lord, along with the direct inspiration of the Holy Spirit. As we feast on the Bible we come to know the character of God. We are infused with faith, hope and love as we spend time in the Word of God. Spending time in scripture under the guidance of the Holy Spirit opens the spiritual communication lines. Prayer time can be an adventure, especially if we get into the habit of easy, spontaneous dialogue with the Lord. I believe if you practice talking to Him conversationally during the day, this portion of your "Miracle Hour" will be even more fruitful.

As you begin this section just say simply, "Lord, please speak to me through Your word today." Open your Bible, browse through it, allow a word or a phrase to catch your attention. Once something catches your eyes, stop there. If, for example, the word, "hope," catches your eye, ponder the meaning of it. Ask the Lord why that word captured your attention. Perhaps the phrase "integrity of heart" will suddenly speak to you. Ask, "Holy Spirit, what do You want to teach me through this word?" Write these reflections in your notebook and continue to meditate on them later. This is a very important record of your spiritual walk. (5 minutes)

(Ps 119:15, Ro 15:4, 2 Ti 3:16, Ro 10:8, Col 3:16, Ps 19:8, Ps 119:130, Ps 119:140, Job 23:12, Ps 119:103, Heb 4:12, Ps 119:9, Jer 23:29, Ro 1:16, Jn 20:31, Eph 6:17, Eph 5:26)

(Our Father, etc.)

9. WAIT FOR THE LORD TO SPEAK:
"Be still before the Lord and wait patiently for Him..." (Psalm 37:7). Use this time simply to listen to the Lord.

How is He encouraging you? Exhorting you? Directing you? Be still and listen. Pray, "Lord, teach me how to be a good listener." This is one of the most special times in the "Miracle Hour." The Lord tells us, *"My sheep listen to my voice..."* (John 10:27). As Christians who sincerely want to progress in our relationship with the Lord, we must find a quiet place, away from noisy distractions, and simply listen to the voice of our Lord. Often it helps to close your eyes. He wants to speak to us more than we want to listen. He is a God of love, and love longs to communicate. Have a pen and note pad handy, and expect Him to speak. The previous steps have built up to this wonderful moment. You have quieted your mind, your heart is open, your conscience is clear, and you are centered on the Lord. And, if you are like most of us, you need a word of encouragement from the Lord. Say, with Samuel, *"Speak, for Your servant is listening"* (I Samuel 3:10). As words or thoughts begin to come into your mind, write them in your notebook. Most probably, it will be the Lord giving you a word of loving encouragement, hope and healing. You will grow in ability to hear Him speak throughout your daily affairs, as you spend quality time in prayer and scripture. Finally, it is also true that love does not require words. God may love you in the silence as well. (5 minutes)

(Dt 30:20, Lk 10:39, Rev 3:20, Ps 95:7, Is 30:21, Hab 2:2, Jn 16:13, Ac 10:19, Pr 8:34, Ps 25:9, Ps 73:24, Mt 13:23)

(Our Father, etc.)

10. **INTERCESSIONS:** *"I urge, then, first of all, that requests, prayers, intercession and thanksgiving be made for everyone..."* (I Timothy 2:1). One of the greatest gifts we can give each other is the gift of prayer. This is the time to pray for other people. Pray for nations

and leaders, pastors and those in authority. Pray for the homeless, aborted babies, the sick and the dying. Pray for those who have no one to pray for them. Pray for your enemies. Pray for your family, friends, and associates. Most importantly, ask the Holy Spirit to bring people to mind. He surely will. Their names probably will continue to come to mind throughout the day, once you make yourself available, because the Lord is always looking for someone willing to pray. As their names come to you, simply lift them to the Lord. Ask Him to help them, to bring them to wholeness, to forgive them, to touch them with His love, to release His power on their behalf. Pray with simple faith, as a little child turning to Daddy, knowing He longs to give you what you want. You might ask, "Lord, what does this person need?" Often an area of need will come to mind. When it does you can say simply, "Lord, Abba, please meet that need." Pray simply, from your heart. Pray, "Father, I pray Your heart's desire be done in their lives." He prompted you to ask, so you can be sure that He will do something about the need! Will you also pray for other people doing their "Miracle Hour," that their prayers will be answered too? *The prayer of a righteous man [and woman] is powerful and effective"* (James 5:16). (5 minutes)

(Is 65:24, Ps 106:23, Eph 1:16, 1 Ch 21:17, Ps 91:15, Is 58:9, Dan 9:4-23, 1 Sa 1:27, 1 Ki 8, 1 Ki 18:37, 2 Ki 19:19, Is 59:16)

(Our Father, etc.)

11. **PETITIONS:** *"Let us then approach the throne of grace with confidence, so that we may receive mercy and find grace to help us in our time of need"* (Hebrews 4:16). This is a time for you to ask the Lord to meet your needs. Get in the habit of asking for everything

throughout the day: parking places, green lights, favor with the boss, etc. This builds a comfortable, free interaction with the Lord that will make it easier to ask, expectantly, when there are serious needs. Do you have certain fears that need to be released? Do you have a weight problem? A health concern? Do you have difficulty with an annoying person? How about holding up to the Lord the long term goals for your life? Be specific. It helps to write down intercessions and petitions, as well as goals, so that when they are answered faith will increase. *"Ask and it will be given to you; seek and you will find; knock and the door will be opened to you. For everyone who asks receives; he who seeks finds; and to him who knocks, the door will be opened."* (Matthew 7:7-8). (5 minutes)

(Mt 21:22, Jn 15:7, Lk 11:9, Jn 14:13, 1 Jn 5:14-15, Ps 34:6, La 2:19, Ps 61:2, Ps 130:1-2, Ps 120:1, Ps 119:169, Ps 119:147, Ps 91:15, Mk 9:23, Ps 62:8)

(Our Father, etc.)

12. **THANKSGIVING:** *"...let us be thankful, and so worship God..."* (Hebrews 12:28). In the closing five minutes of your "Miracle Hour," turn to the Lord and worship Him through your gratitude. Use this prayer as a jumping off point and begin to thank Him spontaneously.

PRAYER OF THANKSGIVING

Give "...thanks to the Father, who has qualified you to share in the inheritance of the saints in the kingdom of light" (Colossians 1:12).

Thank you, loving Father in heaven, for the amazing grace of this "Miracle Hour" with You. Thank You for drawing me to prayer and giving me hunger and thirst for You. Thank You for the joy of surrender, repentance and forgiveness. Thank You for sending the Holy Spirit to teach, guide and counsel me. Thank You for a fresh infilling of the Holy Spirit today, and a release of the gifts of the Spirit. Thank You for sending me people for ministry. Thank You for the fruit of the Spirit working in me: love, joy, peace, patience, kindness, gentleness and self-control. Thank You for encouraging me to ask when I have a need, and helping me to understand the desires of my heart. Thank You for the wonderful gift of praise.

Thank You for breaking the power of old habit patterns and bringing me to deeper conversion. Thank You for the grace to listen to You, believe in You and come to You. Thank You for all the ways You have helped me and intervened on my behalf. Thank You for Your plan for my life, for creating me with a high purpose in mind, for giving me a sense of worth. Thank You for loving me unconditionally and never leaving or forsaking me, no matter what I do. Thank You for being there at all the moments in my life, the rough and the smooth, and bringing me through those moments to a place of maturity and deeper faith.

Thank You for Your living Word that strengthens and empowers me. Thank You for enabling me to rise out of discouragement and walk in joy. Thank You for lifting me up when I fall. Thank You for keeping me in perfect peace, as my mind is stayed on You. Thank You for making all things work together for good as I place my trust in You. Thank You for enabling me to dwell in safety, and protecting me from the snares of the fowler. Thank You for giving Your angels charge over me, to guide me in all my ways. Thank You for blessing me as I come in and go out. Thank You for guiding me and giving me wisdom. Thank You for Your goodness and mercy that follow me wherever I go. Thank You for the grace to lean on Your understanding, not my own. Thank You for enabling me to forsake all negative thoughts today, and only think those thoughts that are healing and uplifting. Thank You for giving me a tongue that speaks healing and life. Thank You for the abundance of your love that casts out all fear. Thank You for fighting for me against my enemies, and even making my enemies at peace with me. Thank You for the grace to choose life today. Thank You for enabling me to keep my heart fixed on You.

Thank You for giving me a spirit of power, love, and a sound mind. Thank You for always causing me to triumph in Christ Jesus, and turning curses into blessings. In You I am more than a conqueror. Thank You for giving me the ability to think Your thoughts and walk steadfastly in Your ways. Thank You for opening the gates of heaven and pouring out blessings. Thank You for supplying all my needs in accordance with Your riches in glory. Thank You for giving me favor with You and with my fellow man. Thank You for freeing me from sickness in body, mind and spirit, and bringing good out of the times when trouble comes. Thank You for giving me a spirit of wisdom and revelation to know the great hope to which l have been called. Thank You for flooding my heart and mind with the light of heaven. Thank You for revealing the immeasurable and unlimited power of God available in me. Thank You for the grace to walk in forgiveness, faithfulness and love. Thank You for my exceedingly growing faith. Thank You for opening my hands to give to the needy, opening my eyes to see the needs of my brothers and sisters, opening my ears to their cry, opening my heart to love the wounded and lost, opening my lips to speak of Your love, and opening my arms to receive others in love. I especially thank You for_____.

Thank You for all the blessings of life: godly ancestors, family, friends, teachers, professional people, clergy and church. Thank You for all who have helped me along the way. Bless them, Lord. Thank You for faith, freedom, health and work. Thank You for science and art and medicine, bicycles and satellites and all the material advancements that improve the quality of life. Thank You for the wonderful gift of my life, exactly the way it is. I embrace it as a priceless gift from You. And I thank You for the greatest gift of all – Your Son Jesus. *"Thanks be to God for this indescribable gift"* (2 Corinthians 9:15).

(Ps 100:4, 2 Co 3:18, Lk 8:39, Ac 13:47, Da 12:3, Ps 126:3, Jn 1:16, 2 Co 9:8, 2 Pe 1:2, 2 Pe 3:18, Phm 7, Ps 91:11, Ps 90:17, Ps 29:11, Dt 23:5, Ps 107:22, 1 Th 5:18)

"You are the God who performs miracles; You display Your power among the peoples" (Psalm 77:14).
Amen!

Lord, please give me Your blessing. Let Your light shine in me today.

About the Author

LINDA SCHUBERT was born Linda Jane Vander Ploeg on November 7, 1937 in Los Angeles, California. She spent her early years with her family on her grandmother's 2400 acre mountaintop ranch on the Northern California coast, where her Dutch father owned the "Bear Trap Lumber Company."

With no Christian training, Linda's earliest experiences of Jesus were feelings stirred in her heart at about age five when she would climb onto an old rope swing tied to an ancient oak tree and sing the beloved children's song, "Jesus loves me." She was to encounter that love at many times of trial after her family lost the ranch and moved from town to town across California where her father sought work as a building contractor. She learned at an early age to shield herself from the hurts of life by building protective walls around her heart. As she looks back on her many mistakes over the years, she reflects, "While my failures were 'legendary,' the love of God was even more legendary. No matter how much I ran from Him, He never let me go." Although she joined the Catholic Church in 1965, she did not have a heart conversion to the person of Jesus Christ until after the death of her stepson, Randy, in 1977, when she fell to her knees and prayed a prayer of surrender with Pat Robertson on the 700 Club television program. At that moment she knew, in the depths of her soul, "Jesus loves ME!" A whole new love for the Christian community and the Catholic Church began to blossom. She knew she would never again have to fight her personal battles alone. The Lord gave her a scripture that was to be her special verse: *"I have set before you life and death, blessings and curses. Now CHOOSE Life..."* (Deuteronomy 30:19). She came to know the Holy Spirit as her comforter, counselor and best friend, and the one who would bring her into that abundant life in which she chose to live. She discovered that with Him she didn't need to hide, or build walls.

Today, Linda travels internationally conducting seminars, retreats and days of renewal. Her popular books on prayer and healing themes have been translated into many languages. She has ministered in the Philippines, Malta, Ireland, North Ireland, Australia, New Zealand, England, Wales, Italy, Switzerland, France, Belize, Mexico, Nigeria, South Africa, Germany, Hungary, Trinidad, Barbados, Grenada, Jamaica, India, Canada and throughout the United States. Other countries are on her upcoming schedule. She has also coauthored nine books with Rev. Robert De-Grandis, S.S.J.

In May 2000 she was appointed to the council of the National Service Committee of the Catholic charismatic renewal in the United States. A member of the Association of Christian Therapists, Linda resides in northern California.

If you are interested in having
Linda come to your area for conferences or
workshops, write, phone or e-mail:

Linda Schubert
Miracles of the Heart Ministries
P.O. Box 4034, Santa Clara, CA 95056

Phone (408) 734-8663
Fax (408) 734-8661

Web Site: www.linda-schubert.com
and
E-mail: linda@linda-schubert.com

Order Form

All of Linda Schubert's resource materials can be ordered online at www.linda-schubert.com.

To order using the form below, send payment to Linda Schubert, Miracles of the Heart Ministries, P.O. Box 4034, Santa Clara, CA 95056; Fax (408) 734-8661, Phone (408) 734-8663, E-mail linda@linda-schubert.com.

Books

____	*Precious Power** .... $ 3.00	____
____	*True Confessions** .... $ 3.00	____
____	*Miracle Hour** .... $ 3.00	____
____	*Miracle Moments** .... $ 3.00	____
____	*Rich in Mercy** .... $ 3.00	____
____	*Miracle Man Handbook** .... $ 3.00	____
____	*Miracle Woman Handbook** .... $ 3.00	____
____	*Healing Power of a Father's Blessing* .... $ 3.50	____
____	*Five Minute Miracles* .... $ 5.00	____
____	*The Gift of Tongues* .... $ 4.00	____
____	*Transfigurations, Places of Prayer with Prof. R. England* $20.00	____

CD's

____	Miracle Hour Prayers (Pray along with Linda) .... $ 8.00	____
____	Double CD Teaching and Miracle Hour Prayers $14.00	____
____	Receive the Gift (Linda's song in English and Spanish) $8.00	____

Total $ _____

California residents add 8.75% tax $ _____

***Shipping $ _____

TOTAL ENCLOSED $ _____

U.S. FUNDS

Visa _____   Mastercard _____

Name on card _____

Expiration date _____

Card # _____

Ship to _____

_____

_____

Phone_____

*For quantity discount of *True Confessions, Miracle Moments, Rich in Mercy, Miracle Hour, Precious Power, Miracle Man Handbook or Miracle Woman Handbook,* use the following chart:

> 1-25 copies .... $3.00 each
> 26-50 copies .... 2.75 each
> 51-99 copies .... 2.25 each
> 100+ copies .... 1.75 each

**Bookstores order Five Minute Miracles from Catholic Book Publishing Co., 77 West End Road, Totowa, NJ 07512, Phone (973) 890-2400. For other books, standard trade discount applies.

***For media rate shipping to U.S. locations, refer to chart below:

> 1 to 5 items add $2.50
> 6 to 20 items add $3.50
> 21 to 35 items add $4.50
> 36 to 50 items add $5.50
> 51 to 70 items add $6.50
> 71 to 100 items add $7.50
> 100+ items add $8.50 per 100

For shipping to other countries contact Linda Schubert.

About the Books

True Confessions . . . **prayers to heal the secrets in your soul.** This is a book about parts of ourselves that we sometimes don't want to admit. And yet, as we bring them to God He opens great fountains of grace. Inviting God into our negative emotions and painful struggles often brings the deepest growth and healing in our lives. Chapters include: When you feel ashamed, in pain, betrayed, angry, afraid, rejected, like a failure, insecure, resentful, stuck, sorrowful, and more.

ISBN 0-9632643-6-2

Rich in Mercy . . . **personal testimony of Linda Schubert.** Charismatic Renewal Services says about this book in their catalog: "You'll grow in appreciation of God's merciful love through this testimony from a well-known charismatic author and speaker. She shares how she searched for love through several failed marriages, how God finally revealed Himself to her and how her relationship with her father was miraculously healed as a result. Read this remarkable story of an ordinary woman's life that was transformed through surrender and grace."

ISBN 0-9632643-3-8

The Healing Power of a Father's Blessing . . . **prayer of a loving father based on Psalm 23.** Foreword by Charles Whitehead, President of International Catholic Charismatic Renewal Services: "It is important because it brings to our attention something we have either forgotten or perhaps never noticed — that words of blessing spoken over us can be life changing. Linda reminds us that blessings can be from God to men, and from men to men. They can be given by our Heavenly Father, and by our human fathers or by someone standing in for them. We would all do well to grasp this message eagerly, and to put it into practice. Then we would not only pronounce life-giving messages over one another — we would also be blessings to one another."

ISBN 0-9632643-2-X

Five Minute Miracles . . . **pray for people with simplicity and power.** "A must read for all who desire to comfort others by praying with them and for those who have not yet dared to desire" (Babsie Bleasdell, Trinidad). "Not just a gem, but a treasure trove of inspiration . . . Linda Schubert demonstrates that arm-around-the-shoulder informality plus let's-pray-about-it compassion can draw five-minute miracles from a God of incandescent love" (John H. Hampsch, CMF).

ISBN 1-878718-08-8

Miracle Hour . . . **a method of prayer that will change your life.** Since publication in 1991, this book has been translated into at least 25 languages. In most cases the translations have been given to various countries with proceeds going to the renewal in those countries.

ISBN 0-9632643-0-3

Transfigurations . . . **places of prayer,** by Prof. Richard England, with Linda Schubert. This "coffee table" style book is rich with colored photos of prayer chapels designed by Prof. Richard England, a distinguished

Maltese architect with international recognition, and recipient of many awards. This book, published by Edizioni LIBRiA in Italy, includes Richard's chapels built on the Island of Malta along with his text, and Linda's prayer experiences within those chapels. Linda says: "I have visited chapels around the world, and none have moved me as much as Richard's chapels." Includes afterword by Robert Faricy, S.J. 85 pages

ISBN 88-87202-06-0

Miracle Moments . . . This book is an invitation to prayer that will help us to see, know and experience the heart of God as He moves within His people. These are simple prayers to reveal a profound love. Some of the topics include: For heart's desire, to redeem failure, to heal damaged relationships, to strengthen marriage, emotional healing, physical healing, release from harmful habits, for times of trouble.

ISBN 0-9632643-5-4

Precious Power . . . **healing flows when we welcome, listen, empower.** The New Testament is rich with examples of the Lord welcoming, listening to, and empowering those who come to Him. Through the precious power of the Holy Spirit He continues this ministry today. As readers prayerfully enter into the examples, reflections and prayers, they can also expect to grow in ability to welcome, listen to and empower others. This is an excellent tool for pastors, counselors and Christian leaders as well as for private use.

ISBN 1-931600-93-7

Miracle Woman Handbook . . . **a Christian guide to a good life.** *Miracle Man Handbook* . . . **a Christian guide to a good life.** Whatever the needs in your life, whatever frustrates you, help is as close as your next heartbeat. God is waiting to release miracle power in you and through you. The thoughts and prayers in these simple handbooks are practical tools to open you to God's plan of action. Bless you on your journey, Miracle Woman and Miracle Man.

Miracle Woman ISBN 1-4276-0561-0
Miracle Man ISBN 1-4276-0560-2

Notes

Notes

Notes

Notes